Cats

Manx Cats

Launch!
An Imprint of Abdo Zoom
abdobooks.com

Leo Statts

abdobooks.com

Published by Abdo Zoom, a division of ABDO, PO Box 398166, Minneapolis, Minnesota 55439.

Launch!™ is a trademark and logo of Abdo Zoom.

Printed in the United States of America, North Mankato, Minnesota.

052019
092019

Photo Credits: Alamy, iStock, Shutterstock, ©Jiaqian AirplaneFan p11/CC BY 3.0

Production Contributors: Kenny Abdo, Jennie Forsberg, Grace Hansen, John Hansen

Design Contributors: Dorothy Toth, Neil Klinepier

Library of Congress Control Number: 2018963140

Publisher's Cataloging-in-Publication Data

Names: Statts, Leo, author.

Title: Manx cats / by Leo Statts.

Description: Minneapolis, Minnesota : Abdo Zoom, 2020 | Series: Cats | Includes online resources and index.

Identifiers: ISBN 9781532127113 (lib. bdg.) | ISBN 9781532128097 (ebook) | ISBN 9781532128585 (Read-to-me ebook)

Subjects: LCSH: Manx cat--Juvenile literature. | Cat, Domestic--Juvenile literature. | Cats--Behavior--Juvenile literature. | Cat breeds--Juvenile literature.

Classification: DDC 636.8--dc23

Table of Contents

Manx Cats

Manx cats love their human families. They always enjoy **company**.

Manx cats are smart. They can open cabinets and doors.

Body

Most Manx cats are called **rumpies**. This is because most Manx cats do not have tails.

Some Manx cats have small tails. They are called **rumpy risers**.

Manx cats have large, round eyes. They have round heads, too.

Manx cats are good jumpers. They have very strong, short legs.

A Manx cat often makes a **chirping** noise. It does not meow.

Care

Manx cats should be brushed once a week. This keeps them from getting hairballs.

Manx cats need litter boxes. The litter box should be placed away from the cat's food and water.

Manx cats also need toys to play with.

Personality

If a Manx cat isn't playing with its toys, it is happy to relax.

Manx cats are smart. They love learning new tricks.

History

Manx cats were first discovered on the Isle of Man. That is an island in the Irish Sea.

They are good at hunting. Manx cats can find and catch mice easily.

Average Weight

A male Manx cat is lighter than a bowling ball.

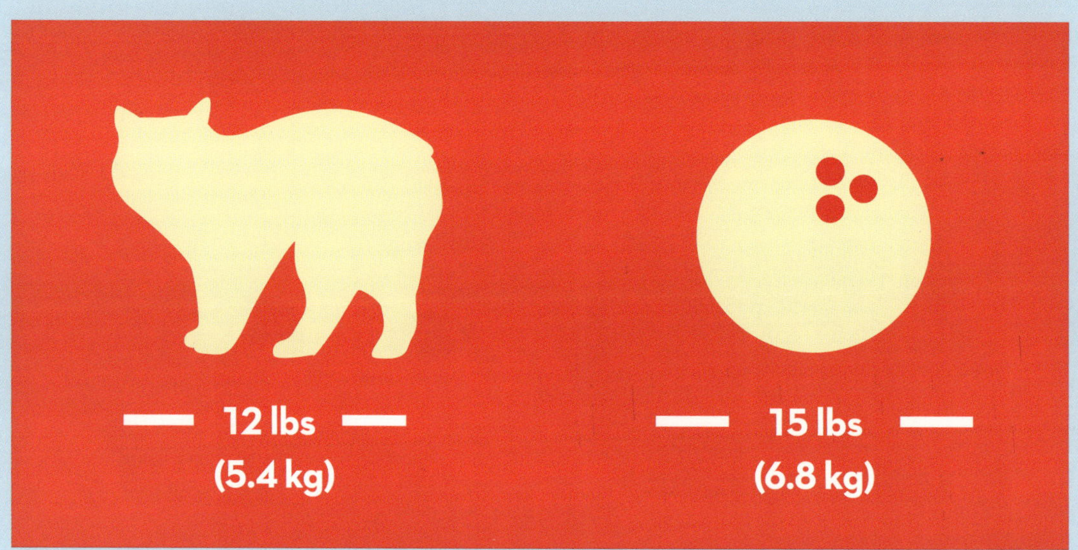

Average Height

A female Manx is longer than a basketball.

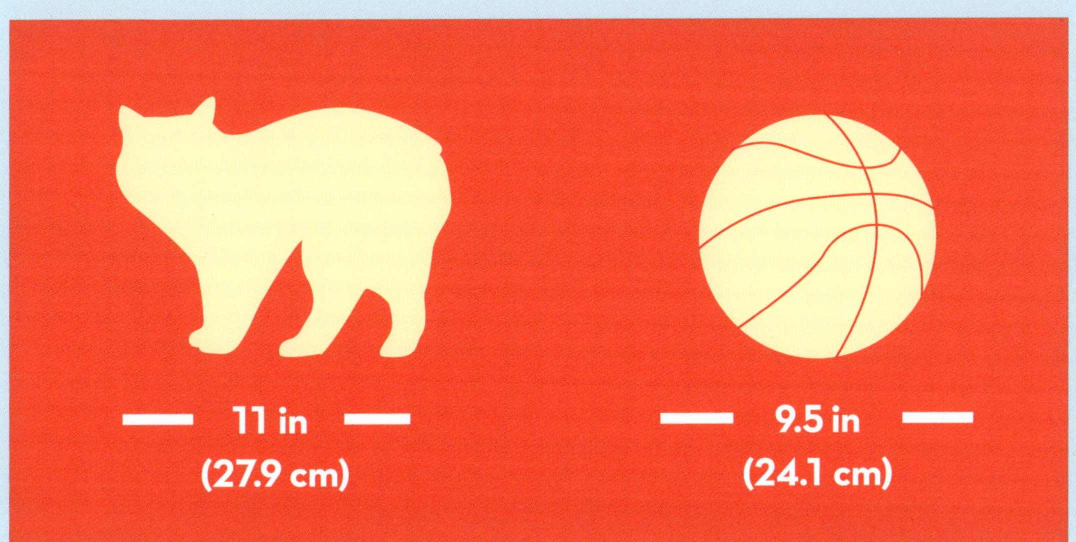

Glossary

chirp – a short, sharp, high-pitched sound.

company – being with another or others.

rumpy – a Manx cat with no tail.

rumpy riser – a Manx cat with a very short tail. It looks like a nub.

Online Resources

For more information on Manx cats here, please visit **abdobooklinks.com** or scan this QR code.

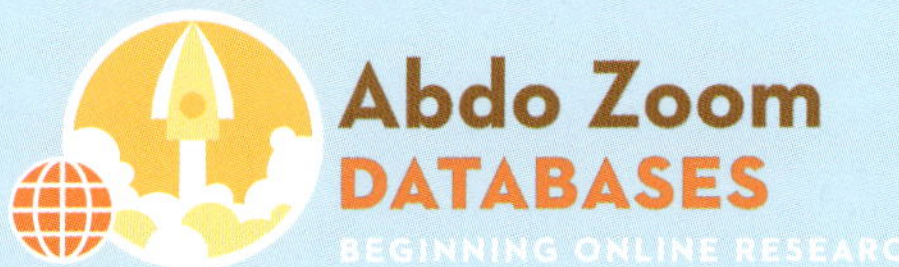

Learn even more with the Abdo Zoom Animals database. Visit **abdozoom.com** today!

Index